Original title:
Glide Like a Swan

Editor: Jessica Elisabeth Luik
Author: Linda Leevike
ISBN HARDBACK: 978-9916-86-371-8
ISBN PAPERBACK: 978-9916-86-372-5

Cascade of Calm

Whispering winds, the trees embrace,
Leaves that dance, a tender trace.
Sky so wide, a tranquil blue,
A world at peace, serene and true.

River's song, a gentle tone,
Stones caressed, a softened moan.
Sunlight filters, golden hue,
Nature's symphony, pure and new.

Meadows stretch, a velvet green,
Birds in flight, a graceful scene.
Linger here, where worries cease,
In this realm, eternal peace.

Hushed Currents

Moonlight shimmers on the stream,
Night unfolds a silent dream.
Stars reflect in water's glaze,
A quiet night, a tranquil phase.

Willows weep with gentle sway,
Whisper secrets of the day.
Softly flows the river's hymn,
As twilight fades, the lights dim.

Owls call softly through the night,
Echoes weave through silver light.
In the stillness, find your rest,
Held by calm, forever blessed.

Woven Through Water

Threads of mist in morning air,
Nature's loom, a vision fair.
Streams that wind through ancient wood,
Binding worlds as water should.

Pebbles dance beneath the tide,
In their path, the currents slide.
Roots entwine in rivers deep,
Secrets held and stories keep.

Echoes of a time long past,
Waves of memories that last.
Woven through the fabric grand,
Water's touch on every land.

Immersed in Grace

Beneath the waves, a quiet place,
Depths that hold a boundless grace.
Ebb and flow of ocean deep,
In the cradle, dreams we keep.

Fishes glide in calm ballet,
Embrace of salt, where shadows play.
Coral realms of colors bright,
Whisper songs from day to night.

Float within the sea's embrace,
Every worry gives to space.
Here in stillness, find release,
Where the waters bring us peace.

Ethereal Presence

In twilight's quiet, shadows twirl,
Wisps of dreams in twilight swirls.
A whisper glides, a secret cry,
In the hush where phantoms lie.

Tender wraiths in moonlight dance,
Glimmering in twilight's trance.
Their whispers soft, like a sigh,
Ghostly echoes 'neath the sky.

Stars above blink slow and wise,
Mirroring the spirits' eyes.
In the silence, they command,
Hushed secrets of a phantom land.

Vessel of Peace

On a tranquil sea, my soul sets sail,
Through whispered winds and evening's veil.
A haven found in silent night,
Serenity's soft, soothing light.

Waves caress with gentle hands,
Lulling tides from distant lands.
In the calm, my heart can heal,
Floating, drifting, still and real.

A vessel where my thoughts find rest,
In quietude, a sacred quest.
Gentle peace in soft embrace,
In this stillness, find your grace.

Gentle Currents

Rivers weave through lush array,
Flowing dreams both night and day.
Whispering leaves in breezy grace,
Nature’s calm, a warm embrace.

Water's song in soft descent,
Soothes the soul with calm intent.
A dance of light on rippling stream,
Glowing visions in a dream.

Feel the pulse of life's own thread,
In the currents, softly led.
River's path, a gentle drift,
Nature's gift, a timeless lift.

Shimmering Grace

Underneath the starlit skies,
Glimmers dance before our eyes.
Touched by light, so pure, so true,
In twilight's glow, they softly flew.

Radiance in gentle sweep,
Promises of dreams to keep.
Soft hues of dawn, a whispered trace,
In the glow, serene embrace.

Mysteries in shadows play,
Night's allure, a calm display.
Shimmering like hope's own face,
In the night, a tranquil grace.

Effortless Drift

In the silence of the dawn,
Dreams take flight on feathered wings,
Flowing gently, ever drawn,
To where the heart's pure river sings.

Whispers in the morning haze,
Guide the soul with tender zest,
Through the twilight's weaving maze,
In search of boundless, peaceful rest.

Stars dissolve in daylight's glow,
As whispers fade to soft refrain,
Time unravels, flowing slow,
In the echoes of the rain.

Nature's chorus, sweet and clear,
Eases worries, dulls the pain,
Effortless, we drift and steer,
Towards a love that shall remain.

Linger in this gentle stream,
Where the past and future blend,
Within the boundless dream,
Effortless, until the end.

Moonlight Dancer

In the hush of midnight sky,
A silken figure takes the stage,
Grace enshrined, to none deny,
Her steps born of page and age.

Stars align in silent cheer,
Casting shadows, soft and bright,
Every move, both far and near,
A testament to pure delight.

Twilight's hand, she does caress,
Spinning tales of joy and woe,
In her dance, the world confess,
Secrets lost in moonlight's glow.

Echoes of her tender flight,
Ripple through the tranquil space,
With each turn, the calm of night,
Holds the beauty of her grace.

In the echoes of her charm,
Underneath the pale moon's glance,
Time stands still, without alarm,
For the timeless, moonlight dance.

Pearls of Stillness

In the calm of morning's breath,
Pearls of stillness softly fall,
Nature whispers life from death,
Echoes of the quiet call.

Waters serenely mirror skies,
Reflecting dreams in silent streams,
Every ripple softly ties,
The heart to nature's silent themes.

Grass sways lightly in the breeze,
Dewdrops cling with tender grace,
In the stillness, one can seize,
A fleeting glimpse of time and space.

Mountains stand in solemn watch,
Guardians of the silent night,
Every peak and valley notch,
Echoes nature's quiet might.

In this haven, souls can rest,
From the world's demanding cruelties,
Finding peace within the crest,
Of life's gentle, tranquil beauties.

Whispers of the Lake

Beside the lake, where lilies lie,
Whispers float and softly weave,
Underneath the twilight sky,
Silent tales the winds conceive.

Ripples dance on water’s face,
Echoes of the past afloat,
Every breeze, a soft embrace,
Whispers words too faint to quote.

Shadows play in twilight's fold,
Secrets glisten in the night,
Every whisper, new and old,
Mingles in the pale moonlight.

Stars reflect in tranquil streams,
Heaven's jewels, a mirrored display,
In the quiet, the world dreams,
Of the whispers, night and day.

Here the heart finds sweet repose,
In the whispers of the lake,
Bearing stories only those,
With a listening soul can take.

Floating Dreams

In twilight hours, our spirits rise,
Upon the clouds, beyond the skies.
We traverse realms where stardust gleams,
In the silence of floating dreams.

Gossamer threads weave through the night,
Guided by a pale moonlight.
Echoes of wishes softly gleam,
Within this space, our souls redeem.

Wandering through celestial streams,
We find the light between the seams.
Here we dance, free from schemes,
In the embrace of floating dreams.

Whispering Serenity

Upon the lake, the lilies sway,
In quiet dance, through night and day.
A whispering wind sings a sweet plea,
Hushed tones of calm, in serenity.

Beneath the pines, where shadows lie,
A whisper floats with a gentle sigh.
The brook's tender tune, the bird’s trills free,
Compose a song in serenity.

In the hush of dawn, 'neath skies soft blue,
The world awakes in stillness true.
A whisper of peace drifts gracefully,
Blanketing all in serenity.

Crystal Ballet

Stars pirouette in midnight skies,
Like dancers with celestial ties.
Each gleam a step in silent play,
A waltz of lights, a crystal ballet.

Snowflakes whirl in winter’s hymn,
Their frosty lace with moonlight trim.
A frozen stage, they softly sway,
In purity, a crystal ballet.

Diamonds glint in morning dew,
Glistening as the dawn breaks through.
Nature's gems join in array,
To partake in this crystal ballet.

Luminescent Lift

Under the veil of night’s embrace,
Moths circle in ethereal grace.
With wings aglow they gently shift,
Lighting the way with luminescent lift.

The fireflies paint their trails in dark,
Leaving behind a fleeting spark.
A dance wherein shadows drift,
Guided by a luminescent lift.

Through twilight's mist, where secrets glean,
Glow worms trace their silver sheen.
Their light, a gift that spirits lift,
With the magic of a luminescent lift.

Celestial Glide

Under starlit skies so wide,
Astral dreams in silence ride,
Galaxies in graceful flow,
Whisper secrets we don't know.

Moonbeams weave a silver thread,
Across the night where dreams are fed,
Planets dance in cosmic flight,
Heaven's canvas painted light.

Nebulas like blossoms bloom,
Shimmer in the velvet gloom,
Constellations mark the way,
Through the endless vast array.

Hearts alight with wander's fire,
Reaching higher, climbing spire,
Through the void, a daring glide,
On the wings of stars we ride.

Celestial bodies, cold and far,
Guide us by their ancient char,
In this endless cosmic tide,
Find our place, and there reside.

Vanishing Ripples

Across the pond, a pebble's leap,
Ripples whisper secrets deep,
Echoes dance in widening rings,
Gentle pulse of softer things.

Reflections shiver, gently break,
In the evening's quiet wake,
Patterns lost, a moment's grace,
Fading ripples leave no trace.

Water holds the fleeting light,
Mirrors day dissolving night,
Whispers fade in twilight's grip,
Echoes of the ripples slip.

Silent waves, the night's caress,
Hold the world in soft duress,
Memories in liquid flow,
Disappear where shadows go.

Ephemeral, the ripples cease,
Quiet fills with tender peace,
Vanishing into the deep,
Pond and sky in tranquil sleep.

Swirling in Stillness

In a world where time is slow,
Swirls of calm begin to grow,
Moments held in gentle spin,
Stillness speaks from deep within.

Leaves descend in silent grace,
Painting spirals through the space,
Nature's breath in soft embrace,
Eternity in this calm place.

Rivers flow without a sound,
Winding paths the earth around,
Harmony in currents found,
Peace in constant, gentle bound.

Clouds in sky like silken thread,
Woven dreams above our head,
Whispers of the dawn in red,
Calmly in the stillness spread.

Life in soft, unbroken stream,
Waking in a tranquil dream,
Swirling in the quiet gleam,
Peaceful as a flowing seam.

Feathered Drift

Feathered flight on breezes low,
Softly sailing, wings aglow,
Clouds of cotton, skies of blue,
Dreams alight in every hue.

Gentle whispers, wind's embrace,
Far above the world's fast pace,
Soaring to the realms unseen,
Floating in a tranquil scene.

Autumn's breath in feathers' fall,
Graceful drift, the quiet call,
Nature's sighs in silent waltz,
Sky and earth in no defaults.

Drift in currents soft and pure,
Hearts aloft in journeys sure,
Weightless in the airy tides,
Gliding high where peace abides.

In the realm of feathered flight,
Morning breaks with gentle light,
Softly drifting, hearts align,
On the wings of dreams divine.

Gentle Passage

On twilight's edge, soft shadows fall,
Whispers of dusk, a beckoning call.
Through silent woods, where moonlight weaves,
A gentle passage, twilight cleaves.

Stars awaken, their dance begins,
Night's soft blanket, pulls us in.
Ethereal paths, light as breath,
In twilight's hold, defying death.

The world, in hush, its secrets keep,
In dreams' embrace, we're led to sleep.
Velvet whispers, in the night,
Guide our souls, with silver light.

Radiant Stillness

In quiet fields, where shadows play,
A radiant stillness, tills the day.
The sun dips low, in golden hues,
Nature sighs, and bids adieu.

A moment seized, where time stands still,
In amber glow, on sapphire hill.
Breathless pauses, catch the heart,
In stillness, where the stars impart.

Whispered secrets, in the wind's sighs,
Eternal calm, beneath the skies.
In twilight's arms, we rest our claims,
Where night and day both lose their names.

Breeze-Kissed Feathers

Breeze-kissed feathers, floating high,
Boundless wings, in azure sky.
In gentle arcs, they weave and twirl,
A dance of freedom, wings unfurl.

Weightless whispers, on the wind,
Through boundless air, their paths begin.
Kissed by sun's soft, warming rays,
Aerial ballet, in the haze.

Skyward dreams, no chains to bind,
In feathered grace, their flight we find.
Ephemeral dance, on open seas,
Bound to freedom, with the breeze.

Graceful Wakes

In dawn's embrace, new light is born,
From night's quiet, day is torn.
Golden rays, the darkness shakes,
A river's life, in graceful wakes.

Ripples spreading, each one led,
By whispers soft, from riverbed.
Nature's chorus, in morning's light,
A symphony, both bold and bright.

Flowing paths, through lands so wide,
Undeterred by time or tide.
In gentle curves, the river snakes,
Life unfolding, in graceful wakes.

Moonlit Passage

In silent woods where shadows play,
The moonlight casts a silver ray.
Whispers float on whispered breeze,
Among the ancient, dreaming trees.

Stars adorn the velvet skies,
Reflect on waters, soft and wise.
Guiding footsteps, soft and slow,
Through paths where only moonbeams glow.

Silent owls in branches high,
Guard the secrets of the sky.
Echoes of the night’s allure,
In moonlit passage, pure and sure.

Mirrored Grace

In waters still, reflections gleam,
A mirrored dance, like dawn's first beam.
Nature's portrait, calm and clear,
Each ripple holds a whispered cheer.

Beneath the skies of azure shade,
Reflections in the lake are laid.
Graceful and serene as air,
The world enchants, beyond compare.

Framing moments, time stands still,
In mirrored grace, the heart does thrill.
Beauty’s mirrored, soft and fair,
A tranquil haven, free from care.

Dreams Afar

Beneath the stars, so far and grand,
Lies a world of dreams, a distant land.
Eyes closed tight, let thoughts take flight,
To places bathed in soft moonlight.

Clouds of silver, skies of blue,
In dreams afar, pure wishes brew.
Mountains tall and rivers wide,
With hope and wonder as a guide.

Travel far on wings of thought,
To lands that waking hours forgot.
In dreams afar, a heart can soar,
To realms of magic, evermore.

Feather-Laden Breeze

A feather floats on gentle breeze,
Dancing softly with such ease.
Nature's breath, so kind and warm,
Embrace the feather, keep it from harm.

Whispers of the meadow sing,
As feather's journey takes to wing.
Graceful flights through skies so wide,
With breeze as constant, loving guide.

Winds of change and currents true,
Carry whispers, fresh and new.
Feather-laden, soft and free,
In breeze's arms, eternity.

Crystalline Path

Amidst the silent, snow-clad trees,
A pathway shimmers, pure and bright.
Steps crunch softly, winter's tease,
Underneath the moon's soft light.

Sparkling jewels in frost abound,
Nature's treasures calmly lay.
A secret beauty to be found,
Guiding hearts along the way.

Whispers of the wind unfold,
In this realm of ice and glass.
Stories of the brave and bold,
Echo through as shadows pass.

Radiant beams, star-charmed guide,
Illuminate the twilight's breath.
On this path where dreams reside,
Life awakens, free from death.

Boundless fields of white expand,
Endless canvas, cold and still.
Crystalline, the world so grand,
In this frozen, silent thrill.

Lightborne Grace

In dawn's embrace, the world alights,
Crimson hues and golden shine.
From night's depths to morning heights,
The dawn's grace, divine.

Gentle whispers, sunlight's kiss,
Waking dreams from slumber's hold.
In this morn, a tranquil bliss,
Miracles, untold.

Light cascading through the leaves,
Nature's symphony in glow.
Every ray, a thread it weaves,
Tales of old, we know.

Moments fleeting, yet so grand,
Ephemeral, this serene sight.
In this grace, the world will stand,
Bathed in gentle light.

Hearts alight with hope anew,
As the day begins its flight.
In this peace, our spirits grew,
With dawn's soft, lightborne might.

Heavenly Drift

Above the clouds, a silver sea,
Endless waves of drifting dream.
Floating realms, so wild and free,
In the sky's serene esteem.

Beneath the stars, a gentle sway,
Celestial whispers, soft embrace.
Night's sweet song, a lullaby play,
In this heavenly, tranquil space.

Softest winds, a soothing touch,
Carry wishes on their wings.
In this drift, we find so much,
Echoes of eternal springs.

Galaxies entwine and dance,
Heaven's canvas, vast and bright.
In their glow, our hearts enchance,
Lost within the starry night.

Through the quiet, endless flight,
Dreams unfold, no bounds to lift.
In this peaceful, ethereal light,
We wander in the heavenly drift.

Subtle Voyage

In a world of whispers, shadows play,
The heart embarks on subtle ways.
Every step, a quiet sway,
In the dusk of fading days.

Through the fields of golden hue,
Barefoot paths, the dreams align.
Voiceless winds, a promise true,
Guiding softly, by design.

Subtle currents, unseen tides,
Carry forth the spirit's quest.
In the stillness, where time hides,
Moments lost and yet, they're blessed.

Silent echoes, memories trace,
Journeys through the woven air.
In this voyage, find your place,
In the truth that lingers there.

With gentle hearts and open mind,
We tread the quiet, endless skies.
Subtle voyage, paths defined,
In the soul's serene reprise.

Serenading Shores

On the edges of the earth, they sing,
Waves in harmony begin to ring.
Songs of old and tales untold,
By the sea, dreams unfold.

Golden sands beneath our feet,
Rhythms of tides, they softly greet.
With every crest, a whisper goes,
In the ebb, a secret flows.

The horizon blushes in morning light,
Sunset embers ignite the night.
Stars like pearls in heaven's sea,
Guide the way, set spirits free.

Moon's embrace, a gentle tide,
Whispers of love, oceans confide.
Shoreline's kiss, a tender plea,
In every wave, a mystery.

Hearts aligned with nature's rhyme,
In serenading shores, we find our time.
Eternal dance of sea and sky,
Where dreams are born and sorrows die.

Veil of Calm

In the hush of twilight's grace,
Calm descends, a soft embrace.
Stars emerge in silent queues,
Whispers in the evening hues.

Veil of calm, the night's retreat,
Every sigh, a gentle beat.
Moonlight drapes the quiet night,
Bathed in silver, pure delight.

Winds of whispers caress the trees,
Nature's lullaby, a tender breeze.
Dreams alight on feathered wings,
In the stillness, the heart sings.

Moments frozen in time's hold,
Stories in the stars, untold.
A tapestry of night unspun,
In the calm, we're all as one.

Solitude's embrace, so dear,
In every quiet, truth we hear.
Within the veil, peace is known,
In the stillness, love has grown.

Twilight Reflection

Sun dips low, a fiery sigh,
Evening colors paint the sky.
Mirror lakes hold twilight's charm,
Nature's orchestra, soft and warm.

Shadows stretch in whispered grace,
Reflections dance on water's face.
Crickets tune their twilight song,
In the dusk, we all belong.

Echoes of the day now wane,
Moments linger, soft refrain.
Silhouettes in amber light,
Transitioning to gentle night.

Candle stars begin to glow,
Silent watch on worlds below.
Moonlight's brush on tranquil streams,
In twilight's pause, we find our dreams.

Silent whispers in the air,
Night's embrace, a tender care.
Reflections of the soul alight,
In twilight's heart, we find our sight.

Mirage of Moonlit Waters

Shimmering beneath the moon's soft gaze,
Waters dance in silver haze.
Mirage of dreams, a liquid light,
Guiding souls through the night.

Ripples echo like whispered songs,
Carrying hopes, where they belong.
Mystic waves, a silent plea,
In their depths, we find the key.

Moonlit paths on waters weave,
Dreams and visions, interleave.
In each ripple, secrets glint,
Messages in moonlight's tint.

Eternal dance of dark and light,
Through the stillness of the night.
A symphony of watery grace,
In mirage, we find our place.

Wisdom flows in gentle streams,
Carrying away the past's dreams.
In moonlit waters, hearts align,
Finding peace, so pure, divine.

Majestic Mirage

Underneath the desert sun, so bright,
Whispers float in shimmering light.
Oasis beckons with its tender mirage,
Hope dances with a secret charge.

Winds weave tales in grains of gold,
Mystic secrets that sands behold.
Dreams emerge from shadows long,
A journey told in silent song.

Mirages play on the weary eye,
Reflections of truth that softly lie.
Contours shift in fluid motion,
A mystic dance of desert devotion.

Journeys carved in ancient rhyme,
Moments etched outside of time.
Footsteps fade in the evening's glow,
Chasing visions that come and go.

In this realm, where real is feigned,
Infinite beauty is forever claimed.
A place where dreams and wishes bind,
The desert holds its secrets kind.

Waltz of Feathers

In twilight skies, they gather vast,
Feathers dance in shadows cast.
A waltz performed with silent grace,
A symphony in this serene space.

Wings that whisper songs of old,
Tales of wonder yet untold.
Unified in their gentle sway,
As night and dreams softly play.

Their flight paints stories with each glide,
In endless waves, they smoothly ride.
Patterns shift in cosmic ballet,
Heaven's chorus by night's display.

Feathers gleam in moon's embrace,
Stars reflect on nature's face.
Harmony in skies, so free,
A testament to what could be.

As dawn begins to break the dark,
Their waltz concludes, leaves a mark.
Echoes linger in the waking day,
Feathers float, then drift away.

Soaring Solitude

High above, where eagles reign,
Solitude is a gentle gain.
Whispers of the winds confide,
In open skies, where dreams reside.

Mountains cradle, valleys deep,
Secrets in their silence keep.
A solitary flight so pure,
Where freedom's essence will endure.

Clouds embrace with tender care,
Wrapping essence in the air.
Horizons beckon far beyond,
A journey where the heart has gone.

Solitary stars show the way,
Guiding where the spirits stay.
In this loft, where souls convene,
Heavenly sights become routine.

Flight of mind and heart combined,
In solitude, the peace we find.
Soaring high, the spirit thrives,
In endless skies, it truly lives.

Velvet Voyage

Moonlight's sheen on velvet seas,
Whispering winds with gentle breeze.
Ships of dreams set out to sail,
On liquid paths where stars prevail.

Night's embrace, so soft and wide,
Guides each vessel with the tide.
Navigating through the dark,
Hearts alight with hope’s own spark.

Waves that shimmer, silver bright,
Reflecting wishes in the night.
Voyagers with spirits keen,
Chasing visions yet unseen.

Journeys marked by starlit trails,
Quiet whispers, silent tales.
Velvet skies and endless blue,
A voyage where the dreams come true.

Morning breaks with golden rays,
Painting skies in new-found praise.
Voyage ends, yet hearts remain,
Tethered to the night’s sweet reign.

Wings of Grace

Upon the air with gentle sweep,
Heavenly currents guide their leap.
In azure skies, they find their space,
Ethereal flight, wings of grace.

Sunlight whispers on feathers bright,
Soft as dreams in the still of night.
Above the world, they chart their place,
Serenely soar, wings of grace.

Horizon calls with endless plea,
Boundless freedom, wild and free.
They dance on high with tender pace,
Majestic rise, wings of grace.

With every pulse, a silent prayer,
They drift on hope through open air.
Infinite beauty they embrace,
Divine and pure, wings of grace.

In sky's embrace, they find their song,
A timeless journey, everlong.
Their flight, a symphony of grace,
To heaven's realm, on wings of grace.

Still Waters Dance

Beneath the surface, whispers deep,
Where silent thoughts and secrets keep.
Mirror calm in sunlight's trance,
Reflecting dreams, still waters dance.

A ripple stirs, a gentle sigh,
The world above mirrored sky.
Falling leaves in autumn's prance,
Become the beat, still waters dance.

Moonlight casts a silver glow,
On tranquil tides that softly flow.
Through night's embrace, a timeless chance,
To witness peace, still waters dance.

Fishes weave in quiet streams,
Caught within their watery dreams.
Nature's rhythm in pure romance,
Perfect harmony, still waters dance.

Yet in the depth, below serene,
Life's mysteries remain unseen.
In liquid realms, life's quiet stance,
Unbroken calm, still waters dance.

Elegance in Motion

Graceful limbs in perfect flow,
Through time and space, they ebb and glow.
Each fluid move, a soft devotion,
Embody art, elegance in motion.

With every step, the world aligns,
A dance of stars, celestial signs.
Unfurling like a poet's notion,
They write the tale, elegance in motion.

Silken threads in twilight spun,
Their dance begins with setting sun.
Eclipsing day with pure emotion,
A tender glim, elegance in motion.

Their shadows paint the twilight sky,
A graceful arc, a silent cry.
In every sway, a new exploration,
Of dreams alive, elegance in motion.

Bathed in light, they glide and spin,
A dance that never will begin.
For in their flow lies true devotion,
To endless night, elegance in motion.

Feathers and Flow

In twilight's glow, they take their flight,
Soft feathers gleam in fading light.
Through dusk they weave with gentle flow,
Their path unknown, where dreams bestow.

Autumn leaves beneath them fall,
Silent whispers, nature’s call.
In embrace of wind they know,
The art of grace, in feathers and flow.

Twined with currents, as they soar,
Boundaries dissolve, they find much more.
A dance of life, both ebb and grow,
In sky they paint, with feathers and flow.

Moonlit journeys, stars aglow,
A symphony that winds bestow.
Midnight’s canvas, shifting, slow,
Their story sings, in feathers and flow.

Each glide and drift, a fleeting kiss,
Of ancient winds, eternal bliss.
In boundless realm where they bestow,
The beauty pure, in feathers and flow.

Heavenly Drift

Through realms of stars we softly glide,
Across the moon's serene divide.
In dreams, the cosmos gently shifts,
On whispered winds, we take our lifts.

The night unveils its twinkling lore,
As shadows dance on silvered floor.
A tapestry of light, unspun,
We drift until the break of sun.

Gossamer Trails

In dawn's embrace, the morning gleams,
We follow gossamer spun dreams.
Their fragile threads weave paths untold,
Through golden fields of marigold.

The air is hushed with secrets fair,
A whisper trails the fragrant air.
On wings of light and dewdrop sailed,
We wander where the heart prevails.

Floating Dreams

Beneath the sky's vast, endless dome,
Our minds begin to freely roam.
In realms where fantasy takes flight,
We drift through endless seas of night.

Stars above like beacons shine,
Guiding hearts through thought's design.
In floating dreams, we find our grace,
A gentle, timeless, boundless space.

Moonlit Passage

Beneath the quiet, watchful sky,
We trace the moonlit path and sigh.
With shadows cast in silver light,
We journey through the whispering night.

Each step a breath against the gloom,
As if we're walking on a loom.
In silken strands, our tales unfold,
In moonlit passage, dreams are told.

Soft Horizon

In the gentle evening glow,
The sky begins its soft embrace,
Colors blend and merge so slow,
As daylight fades without a trace.

Whispers of the night take flight,
Across the edges of the sea,
Stars will soon reveal their light,
In a dance of mystery.

Breezes carry whispers low,
Across the fields so calm,
Nature's story begins to show,
A restful, soothing psalm.

Mountains stand in silent peace,
Guardians of the waning sun,
Time itself seems to cease,
As night and day become as one.

Soft horizon, blend and weave,
A canvas of the earth,
In twilight's arms, we believe,
In the beauty of rebirth.

Feathered Symphony

With the dawn, their song ignites,
A chorus pure and sweet,
Feathered singers reach great heights,
A symphony complete.

In the trees, their notes entwine,
A melody of grace,
Every morning, so divine,
Their music fills the space.

Wings of color, voices blend,
Nature's grand orchestra,
Echoes through the day's extend,
A harmonious spectra.

Solos rise and fall in time,
A cadence born of air,
Each unique, a perfect rhyme,
Intent beyond compare.

Feathered symphony, arise,
With each new dawning light,
Your music, a cherished prize,
To carry through the night.

Harmonious Drift

Upon a river's gentle flow,
A leaf begins its drifting,
Carried where the currents go,
In movements ever-shifting.

Ripples whisper soothing songs,
As waters merge and part,
A journey where the soul belongs,
A voyage from the heart.

Beneath the sun's embracing kiss,
The river's path is clear,
Harmonious in its endless bliss,
Its course both far and near.

Flowing through the valleys wide,
And over rocky bed,
A wanderer on nature's tide,
By unseen forces led.

In the drift, a quiet knowing,
Of peace that's always near,
Moving gently, ever growing,
Without a trace of fear.

Eternal Flight

Wings outstretched against the sky,
They soar in boundless grace,
Eternal flight where eagles fly,
Above this earthly place.

In the realms of endless blue,
Their path is free and wide,
A timeless journey to pursue,
With winds as their guide.

Clouds beneath like oceans fair,
A sea of white and grey,
In heights where all is light and rare,
Their spirits freely sway.

From dawn to dusk, in silence glide,
A dance with no refrain,
In freedom's bound, they choose to bide,
Above the earth's terrain.

Eternal flight, a noble quest,
To touch the very stars,
With hearts that never come to rest,
Beyond the world's bars.

Beyond the Still Waters

In twilight's tender, soothing hues,
Cast upon the silent lake,
Reflections dance in gentle grace,
As day and night partake.

Whispers from the willow boughs,
Cradle dreams in soft embrace,
Echoes of forgotten vows,
Carry hope to timeless space.

Stars alight in twilight's tender care,
Gilding waves with silver threads,
In nature's canvas, rich and rare,
Moments blend, as time unfurls.

Moonlit ripples weave their tale,
Of love, of loss, of yearning,
Beyond the still waters, pale,
Life flows, forever turning.

The quiet heart finds solace here,
In the realm where shadows play,
Where every sigh and silent tear,
Is kissed by the light of day.

Silken Flight

Through the azure skies they soar,
Wings of silk in gentle flight,
Graceful whispers, they implore,
In the sun's caressing light.

Feathered hearts beat in the breeze,
Sculpting dreams in airy glide,
Unseen hands, the currents tease,
Guiding spirits, side by side.

Threads of gold and silver spun,
Weave their path through heavens wide,
In their arcs, by moon and sun,
Mysteries of air confide.

Every gust a whispered story,
Birds of dawn and twilight's glow,
In their wake, the transient glory,
Of life's ever-flowing show.

Above the world, they dare to rise,
Bound by neither earth nor plight,
In the vast, embracing skies,
They find their truth in silken flight.

Ephemeral Phantoms

In twilight, shadows start to drift,
Ephemeral, they weave and wane,
With every breath, their forms they lift,
A dance of dreams that can't remain.

Phantoms pass through ethereal light,
Veils of time the moments bind,
In the stillness of the night,
Whispers echo, left behind.

Fragile as the morning dew,
They rise and fade with dawn's embrace,
Specters, shadows, ever-new,
In their ephemeral grace.

Memories play in fleeting frames,
Echoes of a time now gone,
Yet their presence still remains,
As the night yields to the dawn.

We chase these phantoms in our dreams,
Holding tight to what was there,
But like the moon's reflected beams,
They vanish, dissipate, in air.

Swan Song Whisper

Upon the lake, in twilight's glow,
A graceful creature lingers near,
Softly gliding to and fro,
Her whispered song, so pure, so clear.

Feathers white as morning's light,
Mirror still, the boundless sky,
In her gaze, the dying night,
Meets the dawn's first tender sigh.

With each note, a life's farewell,
Resonating through the calm,
Every ripple starts to tell,
Of her love, her pain, her balm.

On the breeze, the soft refrain,
Swan song whisper, gently played,
A tribute to the joy and pain,
Of the path through light and shade.

And as the final echo fades,
Her form dissolves, in morning's kiss,
In the heart, the memory stays,
Of her silent, swan song bliss.

Silent Navigator

Amid the stars, a vessel sails,
No compass guides, no wind prevails.
A journey charted by silent tides,
Where whispered secrets softly slide.

Through the void, the silence speaks,
In cosmic murmurs, the stardust seeks.
A navigator in tranquil flight,
Guided by the unseen light.

Galaxies spin, in endless dance,
A ballet of chance, a fleeting glance.
The echoes of a distant call,
In silence, we find meaning's thrall.

Beneath the canopy of night,
A voyage through ethereal light.
The silent navigator steers,
Through time's expanse, beyond our fears.

In stillness, worlds begin to form,
In quiet, we escape the storm.
A wordless guide through space profound,
In silence, true direction's found.

Gentle Cascade

Upon the rocks, a whisper sweet,
Where sky and earth in wonder meet.
A symphony of falling mist,
In nature's arms, we coexist.

The gentle song, of water's glide,
In rhythmic grace, it does confide.
A timeless dance upon the stone,
In liquid cadence, we are shown.

Beneath the canopy so green,
A tranquil spirit, pure and clean.
A gentle cascade's endless flow,
In quiet streams, our dreams bestow.

A weaving tale in droplets fine,
A language mute, a sacred sign.
Through ebb and flow, we find our way,
In gentle cascades, night and day.

A mirror to the sky above,
In nature's shield, we find our love.
By gentle cascades, we are healed,
In water's truth, our hearts revealed.

Ephemeral Elegance

A fleeting touch in morning light,
Where dewdrops hang, a fragile sight.
In whispers soft, the flowers sway,
Ephemeral, the dawn's ballet.

The petals kiss the air so thin,
In dawn's embrace, a world within.
A moment's grace, a breath, a glance,
In fleeting time, our hearts ensnare.

The dance of shadows, light and dark,
A fleeting flame, a fleeting spark.
In nature's weave, the thread so fine,
Ephemeral beauty, so divine.

Upon the wind, the whispers ride,
In moments brief, our souls confide.
An elegance that fades too soon,
In twilight's glow, beneath the moon.

A transient tale, of life and death,
In every touch, in every breath.
Ephemeral elegance, we chase,
In fleeting time, we find our place.

Tales of Tranquility

In twilight's glow, the whispers grow,
In hushed tones, the stories flow.
A tranquil realm of dreams untold,
Where hearts and stars their secrets hold.

The gentle lapping of the shore,
In quiet waves, forevermore.
A symphony in softest hues,
In tranquil tales, our spirits fuse.

Beneath the boughs, the breezes sigh,
Where time slows down and spirits fly.
In tales of tranquility we rest,
In nature's lap, we find the best.

A meadow's hush, a sunset's gleam,
In silent moments, life does seem.
A tale spun of the night's embrace,
In tranquil breaths, we find our pace.

In whispered winds, the stories told,
Of life's embrace, of hearts so bold.
In tranquil tales, we find our peace,
In nature's arms, our souls release.

Echoes of Elegance

In halls where whispers weave and twine,
Figures dance in timeless line.
Shadows bow, and shadows gleam,
Echoes sing a silent dream.

Velvet drapes and chandeliers,
Tales they've told through countless years.
Footsteps light on marble pure,
Graceful, fleeting, ever sure.

Waltzing through the ghostly night,
Candles casting softer light.
Memories held in jeweled clasp,
Lost in elegance we grasp.

Inner Reflections

Quiet streams of thought unfold,
In the heart, a story told.
Echoes from the mind's abode,
Journey on a winding road.

Mirrors show the depth inside,
Fears that we may try to hide.
Hopes that glimmer, doubts that fade,
In our secrets, we're arrayed.

In the silent, still embrace,
Facets of our being trace.
Wisdom growing day by day,
Inner light to guide our way.

Feathered Harmony

Dawns break with a song so pure,
Birds in chorus, hearts allure.
Wings that beat in rhythmic sound,
Nature's symphony unbound.

In the treetops, melodies,
Whispers float on gentle breeze.
Feathers painting morning skies,
Graceful arcs where freedom lies.

Harmony in flight and tune,
Underneath the waning moon.
Every note and every beat,
Nature's music, wild and sweet.

Sky and Stream

Vast expanse of azure grace,
Blissful heights our thoughts embrace.
Clouds that drift in cotton form,
Eternal calm against the storm.

Ripples dance on streams below,
To the sea, they softly flow.
Mirroring the sky above,
In their depths, the stars they love.

Unity of sky and stream,
Boundless whispers, dawn's pure gleam.
On this path, our spirits glide,
In their solace, worlds collide.

Harmonious Ripples

In twilight's tender embrace,
Where water meets the sky,
Soft ripples trace their course,
Under a moonlit sigh.

Stars whisper ancient tales,
To the calm and knowing sea,
Each wave a gentle caress,
In boundless love they're free.

A harmony of light and dark,
Dances on the tide,
Eternal whispers of the night,
Where secrets gently bide.

The breeze a tender lullaby,
Plays on nature's strings,
Harmonious ripples beckon,
To listen is to dream.

In this serene communion,
Where earth and heavens meet,
The song of life in ripples,
Is pure and bittersweet.

Winged Embrace

Beneath the sky so vast,
A world of dreams takes flight,
Wings spread wide in freedom,
To dance with endless light.

Each feather tells a story,
Of journeys far and near,
In a winged embrace, they whisper,
Of love both strong and clear.

Caressing winds of change,
They soar beyond the dawn,
With hearts alight with courage,
To greet the coming morn.

Their dance a silent melody,
Of grace and boundless might,
In the winged embrace of destiny,
They vanish into night.

The skies hold their secrets,
In an infinite, tender song,
A winged embrace forever,
Where they belong.

Tranquil Flight

In fields of endless green,
Where whispers greet the day,
A tranquil flight begins,
As shadows softly sway.

With wings like velvet whispers,
They glide through azure skies,
In a dance of silent beauty,
Where every heart complies.

Breathing in the morning dew,
A symphony of wings,
They paint the air with grace,
While nature softly sings.

In the quiet of the morn,
Their flight a gentle grace,
A moment stilled in time,
In nature's warm embrace.

Tranquility is found,
In every rise and fall,
A flight that whispers peace,
To one and all.

A Symphony of Sails

Across the vast horizon,
Where sea and sky converge,
A symphony of sails,
Begins its endless surge.

Like ghosts upon the water,
They drift in silent dance,
With every wave's caress,
Their spirits find romance.

In the golden light of dawn,
They shimmer, pure and bright,
A fleet of dreams set free,
In the morning's tender light.

The ocean's breath their muse,
Each sail a note of grace,
Together they compose,
A song that time can't erase.

A symphony of sails,
In concert with the breeze,
They sing of boundless journeys,
And endless, gentle seas.

Celestial Drift

Stars cascade through night's black veil,
Dancing in a cosmic tale.
Silhouettes in twilight's mist,
Whispers guide the heavens' list.

Moonlight's touch on sleeping seas,
Breezes whisper ancient pleas.
Galaxies in soft embrace,
Time and space, a slow retrace.

Planetary orbs align,
In the vast expanse, so fine.
Journey through the endless night,
Lost in wonder, pure delight.

Nebulae in colors bright,
Guardians of eternal light.
Constellations draw a map,
In the sky's spectacular lap.

Meteors streaking, silent cries,
Tracing paths through boundless skies.
In the boundless, hearts uplift,
Endless dance of celestial drift.

Heron's Journey

Waters still, a mirror clear,
Heron's wings spread far and near.
Glistening in dawn's embrace,
Graceful paths it’s set to trace.

Through the reeds, it glides serene,
Nature's shadow, seldom seen.
Silent as the morning dew,
Painting skies in shades of blue.

River’s curve, a gentle guide,
Where the ancient spirits bide.
Every flap, a whispered song,
In this realm, where spirits belong.

Mountains echo, valleys sigh,
Where the land and selva lie.
Heron’s call in morning's gleam,
Wakes the world from silent dream.

Journey taken, wisdom earned,
Every pond and bay discerned.
Beneath the skies, it takes its turn,
Heron's tale in life’s great churn.

Grace on the Water

Ripples form where raindrops land,
Traced by nature's gentle hand.
Swans glide on mirrored lakes,
In their wake, tranquility wakes.

Lilies float in quiet calm,
Guardians of a soothing psalm.
Boats drift by on paths untold,
In their journeys, secrets hold.

Moon reflects on waves so slight,
Casting dreams in silver light.
Whispered breeze in early dawn,
Carries tales the heart has drawn.

Feathers stroke the water’s face,
Silent steps of boundless grace.
Fishing lines in twilight's glow,
Stories of the depths below.

Morning breaks with golden hues,
Nature’s canvas born anew.
Grace on water, soft and bright,
In this realm of pure delight.

Feathers in Flight

Wings unfurl in morning breeze,
Gliding over forest seas.
Feathers in the sunlight blaze,
In the sky, a fiery maze.

Clouds above, a boundless stage,
Nature's dancers disengage.
Songs of freedom, echoes bright,
Feathers take to endless flight.

Hawks soar high with piercing gaze,
Sparrows sing in morning's rays.
Eagles claim the blue domain,
Every flight, a sovereign claim.

Autumn leaves with birds descend,
Silent whispers, heavens send.
From the nest, to boundless blue,
Journeys marked by skies they flew.

Evening falls with shadows deep,
Birds to roost, the world asleep.
In dreams they soar, hearts alight,
By the moon’s soft silver light.

Gossamer Trails

In twilight's gentle, fading glow,
Where dreams in whispered breezes flow,
The gossamer threads of night unveil,
A secret path where stars prevail.

The moonlight weaves its silver song,
Through branches where night birds belong,
Soft whispers of the twilight pale,
Lead us on these gossamer trails.

Between the realms of sleep and wake,
A journey through dreams we undertake,
In starlit fields where shadows play,
We wander till the break of day.

Each step a ballet, light and free,
Across the night's vast, silent sea,
Ethereal paths that time entails,
Beckon us on gossamer trails.

For in the velvet night we find,
The boundless beauty of the mind,
A canvas where our spirit sails,
Forever on these gossamer trails.

Aquatic Serenade

Beneath the waves where dreams reside,
In oceans deep, the secrets hide,
A world where silent echoes play,
An aquatic serenade each day.

The dolphins dance through liquid skies,
With songs that in the currents rise,
A melody of life unfurled,
Within the silent blue sea world.

Coral reefs like cities stand,
With vibrant hues that grace the sand,
Each ripple hums a soft brigade,
Part of the aquatic serenade.

The gentle sway of kelp so green,
A ballet in the deep unseen,
The sea, a vast and mystic glade,
Sings an endless serenade.

Through caverns dark where light refrains,
Echoes of the ocean's strains,
In every crest and every wave,
An aquatic serenade to crave.

Ephemeral Grace

Light as a whisper, the morning dew,
Glimmers on petals, fresh and new,
An instant caught in nature's space,
A moment of ephemeral grace.

The sunlight dances on the stream,
A fleeting glow, a golden beam,
Each fragile ray that lights the face,
Imbued with such ephemeral grace.

Blossoms bloom and petals fall,
As seasons whisper nature's call,
Beauty fleeting, time can't erase,
A testament to grace in space.

The butterflies, with wings so fair,
Gently glide through summer's air,
Their path a poem, soft to trace,
Moments of ephemeral grace.

In every breath, in every sigh,
The transient beauty of the sky,
We find a world we can embrace,
Alive with such ephemeral grace.

Dusk's Enchantment

As daylight sinks in twilight's hue,
The sky unfolds a softer blue,
In shadows deep and stars alight,
Unfolds the dusk's enchanting night.

The whispering winds, the rustling leaves,
In evening's arms the world reprieves,
Each twinkling star a silent sprite,
Dancing in dusk's enchantment bright.

Hues of crimson, gold, and jade,
Paint the sky as light fades,
With every shade that courts the night,
We bask in dusk's enchanting light.

The night birds sing their twilight tunes,
As orchid skies embrace the moon,
A world transformed, so soft, so slight,
Under dusk's enchanting sight.

In this serene and magic time,
Where dreams and reality intertwine,
The heart finds peace in starlit flight,
Amidst the dusk's enchanting night.

Silent Reflections

In the quiet of the dawn,
Where whispers softly nest,
Thoughts on wings are drawn,
Within the mind's quiet fest.

Shadows dance in morning light,
Memories gently traced,
Silence holds the stars of night,
In moments still, embraced.

On tranquil lakes they glide,
Reflections pure and deep,
Secrets they confide,
As silent dreams now seep.

Ephemeral as morning mist,
These thoughts so lightly tread,
In silence, life is kissed,
By things unsaid, unread.

In the stillness of the heart,
Where reflections find their grace,
Silent echoes part,
Leaving naught but open space.

Majestic Pathways

Through ancient woods they wind,
Paths of lore untold,
Majestic trees we find,
Guardians of the old.

Pebbles soft beneath our feet,
Nature's whispers close,
Each step a solemn beat,
Where the heart freely goes.

Sunlight filters through the leaves,
Casting golden threads,
Each ray gently weaves,
A dance above our heads.

Mountains touch the sky,
With peaks that whisper dreams,
In silence, they comply,
Amidst sun's gentle beams.

Majestic pathways call,
Through valleys, over hills,
In nature's quiet thrall,
We move, as spirit wills.

Timeless Stream

A stream flows ever bright,
In whispers soft and clear,
Its journey, day and night,
To hearts it calls sincere.

Stones it smooths with care,
In ceaseless, gentle flow,
Ancient tales it bears,
Of times we long to know.

Flowing thoughts to sea,
Through tranquil, meandering way,
Timeless, wild and free,
It guides without delay.

Reflecting skies above,
In shimmering, fluid dance,
Boundless as our love,
Unyielding in its trance.

In the stream's embrace,
Echoes blend and glide,
Timeless, in its grace,
Forever by our side.

Serenity in Flight

Wings spread wide in flight,
Over fields of gold,
In the morning light,
Stories still untold.

Sky's embrace so vast,
A canvas pure and blue,
In each breeze a past,
Old and ever new.

Feathers smooth and bright,
With whispers of the wind,
Guiding through the night,
Where dreams and stars ascend.

Circling high above,
With grace beyond compare,
In every soaring dove,
Peace is found midair.

Serenity in flight,
Through dawn's early hue,
In silence, hearts take flight,
To realms where skies renew.

Hushed Horizons

The sun sets low, a brushstroke blend,
Soft whispers in the sky extend,
Gold and pink, a gentle sigh,
Hushed horizons bidding bye.

Mountains dye in twilight's hue,
Stars ignite, so bright, so true,
Night's embrace, a velvet glove,
Promises of dreams above.

Winds grow still, the world serene,
Silent moments, pure and clean,
Nature's lullaby, sweet and mild,
Softly cradles night's own child.

Moonlight drapes the earth in silk,
Shadows drink the evening's milk,
Eyes of night watch calm and bright,
Hushed horizons, soft and light.

Graceful Sweep

Swirling leaves, a dance of grace,
Nature dons her autumn lace,
Gold and crimson, every hue,
Graceful sweep under skies of blue.

Winds caress, the branches bow,
Silent whispers, here and now,
Elegance in fleeting chore,
Graceful sweep forevermore.

Rivers flow with gentle care,
Mirrors of the skies they bear,
Ripples speak in silent gleam,
Graceful sweep of nature's dream.

Mountains rise with somber might,
Guardians of the day and night,
Silence reigns in lofty keep,
Graceful is their sweeping sweep.

Reflective Dance

Moon's reflection on the lake,
Dreamlike ripples weave and wake,
Stars above and stars below,
Reflective dance in gentle flow.

Trees converse in shadows deep,
Guardians of the secrets they keep,
Whispers of an ancient trance,
Join the night's reflective dance.

Clouds like silk drift in the night,
Blanket of the softest light,
Mirrored in the water's trance,
Echoing the calm expanse.

Time stands still in nature's clasp,
Quiet moments we gently grasp,
In this tranquil, moonlit stance,
We join the night's reflective dance.

Silhouette on Water

A lone tree's shadow, long and thin,
Falls gently on the river's skin,
Against the sunset's wary glow,
Silhouette on water flows.

Cranes in flight, their wings spread wide,
Glide like whispers on the tide,
In the twilight's golden light,
Silhouettes in fading sight.

Fisher's boat, a quiet drift,
Ripples part and calmly lift,
Evening's peace, its shadows caught,
Silhouette on water sought.

Moon ascends, the night's soft queen,
Gently touches silver sheen,
In her gaze, the waters shiver,
Silhouettes forever quiver.

Aglow on the Pond

Golden rays on water's face,
Whispers of the dawn embrace.
Lilies drift in tranquil dance,
Nature's quiet, soft romance.

Ripples echo 'cross the way,
Sunlight's shimmer here to play.
Moment frozen, peaceful bond,
Hearts aglow upon the pond.

Dragonflies in silent flight,
Mirrored dreams in soft daylight.
Gentle breezes weave their song,
Harmony where we belong.

Cattails sway in gentle breeze,
Morning's breath with tender ease.
Time stands still, a world beyond,
Life reflected on the pond.

Moon will rise, replace the sun,
Nighttime's cloak when day is done.
Stars will twinkle, lights respond,
Timeless beauty on the pond.

Effortless Grace

Butterflies in morning's glow,
Dance above where flowers grow.
Wings that flutter, tales they trace,
Nature's gift of effortless grace.

Stream flows gently by the tree,
Whispered secrets, flowing free.
Life's deep rhythm sets the pace,
Guided by its effortless grace.

Swallows dart across the sky,
Arcs of freedom, soaring high.
Boundless, endless, in their chase,
Carried by the breeze's grace.

Willow branches, soft and low,
Bend to earth with gentle flow.
Nature’s story softly place,
Written with such effortless grace.

All around, with silent mirth,
Every creature claims its worth.
In the stillness, find your space,
Connect with life’s effortless grace.

Echoes in the Breeze

Whispers carried, winds so free,
Messages for you and me.
In the leaves, a song is played,
Echoes in the breeze conveyed.

Memory in every gust,
Dreams and thoughts in breezes trust.
Nature's voice, a vast reprise,
Life's secrets float on the breeze.

Mountains stand and valleys low,
Carry tales the winds bestow.
Listen close, you'll find the keys,
Wisdom in those gentle breezes.

Fields of gold and skies of blue,
Touched by whispers, fresh and true.
Every moment's like a tease,
Endless echoes in the breeze.

Stand and breathe beneath the sky,
Feel the world as time goes by.
Let your spirit find its ease,
Lifted by the calmest breeze.

Ballet of the River

Water flows, a dance so pure,
Graceful movements, ever sure.
Moonlight glints on currents' glide,
Ballet of the river wide.

Pebbles whisper, 'neath the stream,
Ancient voices, twilight dream.
In its journey, none denied,
Rivers flow, its dance complied.

Leaves afloat, in twirling spin,
Joined by fish, like silken fin.
Symphony by nature's guide,
Dancing to the riverside.

Whirlpool turns in mystic spin,
Cycles of the world begin.
Flowing onward, side by side,
Part of nature's endless ride.

Stars above in mirrored show,
Reflect the waters' gentle glow.
Silent night, with none beside,
Enjoy the river's endless tide.

Silent Ripples

In the stillness of the night,
Where dreams take gentle flight,
Ripples dance upon the lake,
Silent whispers in their wake.

Moonlight casts a silver hue,
Painting visions faint yet true,
Stars reflect on waters calm,
Nature's breath a soothing psalm.

Leaves above in soft ballet,
Wind and water's tender play,
Time seems lost within these drifts,
Silent ripples, nature's gifts.

Echoes of a distant past,
Through the night, forever last,
In the quiet, hearts find peace,
Silent ripples never cease.

Memories on the water glazed,
In the night, the soul is phased,
Silent ripples, life’s own mark,
Twilight whispers in the dark.

Through Glistening Shadows

Beneath the canopy's embrace,
Shadows flit in gentle grace,
Glistening as the sunbeams pass,
Fleeting moments through the glass.

In the forest's hidden way,
Where light and darkness gently sway,
Steps are careful, breaths are slow,
Through glistening shadows, we follow.

Whispers of a world unseen,
In the twilight's soft, serene,
Nature's secrets softly shared,
In the shadows gently bared.

Fragile dewdrops catch the light,
Turning darkness into sight,
Through the shadows, bold and bright,
Life emerges, a wondrous flight.

In the dance of dark and gleam,
Dreams are born, they softly stream,
Through the shadows, hope ignites,
Glistening, the heart takes flight.

Effortless Whisper

Softly does the morning rise,
Whispers trace the twilight skies,
Effortless as breath of dawn,
As the night is gently drawn.

Murmurs of a waking world,
Nature's beauty, dreams unfurled,
Winds caress the early bloom,
Kissing petals, chasing gloom.

In the quiet of the morn,
Hope is vibrant, gently born,
Whispers through the fields of green,
Painted hues in golden sheen.

Voices of the earth and sky,
Join in quiet lullaby,
Effortless, the whispers blend,
Nature's song, no start, no end.

In these moments, pure and true,
Life's own whispers, found anew,
Effortless, they weave and sway,
Guiding gently through the day.

Floating Elegance

Upon the breeze, they softly glide,
Butterflies in springtime's pride,
Floating elegance, they show,
In the sunlight, gently glow.

Petals float upon the stream,
Carried as if in a dream,
Graceful arcs, a ballet grand,
Nature’s beauty, hand in hand.

Birds in flight, with wings so spread,
Painting skies in hues of red,
Floating elegance up high,
In an endless azure sky.

Clouds that drift and reshape,
Worlds upon the sky they drape,
Effortless in their embrace,
Floating elegance, time and space.

Moments captured, fleeting grace,
In this tranquil, gentle place,
Floating elegance takes hold,
Stories in the breezes told.

Milton Keynes UK
Ingram Content Group UK Ltd.
UKHW010308160824
447029UK00006BA/48

9 789916 863718